Collins

Aiming for Level
Writing

3

Keith West

Series editor: Grant Westoby

William Collins' dream of knowledge for all began with the publication of his first book in 1819. A self-educated mill worker, he not only enriched millions of lives, but also founded a flourishing publishing house. Today, staying true to this spirit, Collins books are packed with inspiration, innovation and practical expertise. They place you at the centre of a world of possibility and give you exactly what you need to explore it.

Collins. Freedom to teach.

Published by Collins
An imprint of HarperCollins Publishers
77-85 Fulham Palace Road
Hammersmith
London
W6 8JB

Browse the complete Collins catalogue at
www.collinseducation.com

10 9 8 7 6 5 4
ISBN 978 0 00 731686 1

British Library Cataloguing in Publication Data.
A Catalogue record for this publication is available from the British Library.

Commissioned by Catherine Martin
Design and typesetting by Jordan Publishing Design
Cover Design by Angela English
Illustrations by Jerry Fowler
Picture research by Gemma Wain
Printed in China

Acknowledgements

The publishers gratefully acknowledge the permission granted to reproduce the copyright material in this book. While every effort has been made to trace and contact copyright holders, where this has not been possible the publishers will be pleased to make the necessary arrangements at the first opportunity.

Extracts from *Mr Gum and the Biscuit Billionaire* by Andy Stanton, published by Egmont Books Ltd. (pp12,16); extract from *Dark Detective* by J.A.C. West, published by Badger Publishing (p52); extract from *Spook Manor* by David Orme, published by Badger Publishing (p52); extract from 'The Sailor' by Michael Owen, from *Spell Poems*, published by Weld Educational Books (p61).

The publishers would like to thank the following for permission to reproduce pictures in these pages:

Adam Dodd/istockphoto (p6); Peter Close/istockphoto (p7t); Diane Diederich/istockphoto (p7b); Jim Arbogast/Getty Images (p8t); istockphoto (p8b); Jonathan Larsen/istockphoto (p9); Andrew Drysdale/Rex Features (p10t); Jim Kruger/istockphoto (p10b); Semenscu Bogdan/istockphoto (p11); Olivier Blondeau/istockphoto (p12); istockphoto (p13); Mark Evans/istockphoto (p19); Terry Morris/istockphoto (p20t); Frances Twitty/istockphoto (p20b); istockphoto (p21t); Steven Hayes/istockphoto (p21b); Emilia Stasiak/istockphoto (pp25l, 25r); istockphoto (p26); John Bell/istockphoto (p28); istockphoto (p29); Betsy Dupris/istockphoto (p32); John Pitcher/istockphoto (pp34, 35); istockphoto (p36); Daniel Bobrowsky/istockphoto (p37); Action Press/Rex Features (p40); Ken McKay/Rex Features (p41); Dion van Huyssteen/istockphoto (p42); istockphoto (p46t); Ian Peters/istockphoto (p46b); Terry Healy/istockphoto (p47); Steve Luker/istockphoto (p48t); Stephen Patterson/istockphoto (p48b); Shaun Lowe/istockphoto (p52t); Nina Matthews/istockphoto (p52b); Susan Trigg/istockphoto (p53); istockphoto (p54); Lee Pettet/istockphoto (p57); istockphoto (60t); George Pchemyam/istockphoto (60b); Rebecca Ellis/istockphoto (61); Claudia Dewald/istockphoto (p62t); Chris Schmidt/istockphoto (p62b); istockphoto (p63).

Contents

3DH

Chapter 1

AF6 Write with technical accuracy of syntax and punctuation in phrases, clauses and sentences

This chapter is going to show you how to

- Recognise a sentence
- Use capital letters
- Use full stops, question marks and exclamation marks
- Recognise speech in stories.

What's it all about?

You will be able to write using sentences.

Getting you thinking

A sentence is a group of words that make sense.

Look at the two sentences below.

> Lord Lazybones could never tie his shoelaces.

> Mrs Snob fell a cowpat.

Which sentence does not make sense?

How does it work?

The first sentence makes sense and is correct. The second sentence does not make sense; it is wrong. One word can make the sentence correct… Can you think of this word?

> Mrs Snob fell **into** a cowpat.

(The word 'into' would make the sentence correct. You might have thought of other words that would also make the sentence correct – such as **onto**, or **on**.)

Now you try it

Copy out the following sentences. Tick the sentences that make sense and complete the sentences that do not make sense.

1 My dad is.

2 My friend wears a hoodie.

3 I saw a ghost last week.

4 There were two.

5 I support Arsenal.

6 The sun shines.

7 The sun shines on my.

8 The animal growled.

9 He dug his.

10 You are brave.

11 Shirley was a… .

You can see from the sentences above that you start a sentence with a capital letter and end with a fullstop.

Getting you thinking

You need to start sentences with a capital letter.

Example:
The footballer fell into the mud.

This sentence makes complete sense. It starts with a capital letter.

How does it work?

When you use a capital letter in the right place, people will know you are starting a new sentence. It makes your work easier to read.

Now you try it

The writer was in a hurry and he has not used capital letters in his sentences. Read through his writing and put in the missing capital letters.

he knew they were after him. they wanted to steal the key. the key would unlock the treasure chest. he must hide the key.

Development activity

Capital letters must also be used to begin a person's name.

Examples: Oliver, Ruth.

Capital letters are also used for place names.

Examples: Australia, London, Colchester.

Capital letters must also be used for

- the days of the week: for example, Sunday.
- the months of the year: for example, May.
- names of events: for example, Yom Kippur.

Copy out these sentences and put capital letters in the right places.

1   the bald man's wig blew away.
2   joe sneezealot sneezed in paris.
3   this christmas will be a fun time.
4   christina and joanne are friends.
5   we travelled from pembroke
    to coventry.
6   the man who ate six pies was
    john gobbledown.

Getting you thinking

Full stops are used at the end of a sentence, unless the sentence is a question sentence (?) or the sentence needs an exclamation mark (!).

Example:
The thief stole money.

Full stops tell the reader that you have finished a sentence.

The silly writer was in a hurry again. This time he did not use full stops. Read through his writing and put in the missing full stops.

The wolf howled at the moon A man hid in the forest He was frightened He had never heard a wolf before

How does it work?

Question marks and exclamation marks are sometimes used instead of full stops.

Example: Do you understand this work?
I am glad you do!

Now you try it

What type of punctuation mark does each sentence need?

1   Look sharp, lad
2   How many cats have you got
3   I've lost my homework

Development activity

Most of your sentences will end in full stops. If you use a one-word sentence or a command, you will normally need an exclamation mark. Use question marks when you ask questions.

Copy out the following sentences and end them with full stops, exclamation marks or question marks.

1   Do you think it will snow today
2   Hey, you
3   Stop at once
4   Have you seen the wolf
5   Did you go near the haunted house
6   Wow, that's good

Check your progress

LEVEL 2   I can use full stops

LEVEL 3   I can mostly use full stops, exclamation marks or question marks

Getting you thinking

Have you noticed how speech is set out in stories?

In *Mr. Gum and the Biscuit Billionaire* Polly has just seen a gingerbread man, who is carrying lots of money in a tin.

'Hello,' said the little weirdo, skipping over to where Polly sat, 'I'm Alan Taylor.'

'I'm Polly,' replied Polly in wonder. 'Are you from Fairy Dream Land where the rivers run with lemonade and the streets are paved with unicorns?'

'Please don't make fun of me,' said Alan Taylor. 'Haven't you ever seen a gingerbread man with electric muscles before?'

How does it work?

If speech is set out correctly, it makes it easier to understand when people are speaking.

Now you try it APP

Put in speech marks where you think people are actually speaking.

1   Hello, said the old lady. Can you help me cross the road?

2   My name is Cliff Edge, said the funny little man.

3   Where am I? asked the boy, as he woke from a deep sleep.

4   The alien grunted, Is this planet Earth?

Level Booster

LEVEL 2

- I can write using capital letters
- I can write using full stops
- I can recognise a sentence

LEVEL 3

- I can start sentences with capital letters
- I can end sentences with full stops, question marks and exclamation marks
- I can use speech marks

LEVEL 4

- I can use commas in lists
- I can punctuate and set out written speech
- I can use commas like brackets

Chapter 2

AF5 Vary sentences for clarity, purpose and effect

This chapter is going to show you how to

- Recognise the present and the past tense in stories
- Turn the present into the past
- Join sentences together.

What's it all about?

You will be able to recognise sentences using the past and present tense.

Getting you thinking

Have you noticed some stories use <u>was</u> and others use <u>is</u>?

Look at the example below. It is from *Mr Gum and the Biscuit Billionaire.*

> A little figure appeared over the top of Boaster's Hill. It was the strangest little man Polly had ever pointed her eyes at. For a start, he was only 15.24 centimetres tall. And he was made entirely out of gingerbread, with raisins for eyes. And he had electric muscles so he could walk around like you or me, and blue sparks came of him whenever he moved. And what's more, he carried an enormous biscuit tin and it was stuffed full of money.

How does it work?

This story is written as if everything has happened in the past. You can tell it is in the past because the word 'was' is used a lot.

Now you try it

1   Look through the story and count up the amount of times 'was' is used.

2   Write about something that has happened to you in the past. Use just three or four sentences.

Development activity **APP**

Here is another story. This one is written in the present, as if it is happening now.

Eric and the Red Dragon

Eric <u>can</u> see the red dragon. It <u>is</u> ugly and big and scary. The red dragon <u>opens</u> its large mouth and <u>breathes</u> fire. The fire <u>is</u> coming straight towards him. Eric <u>is</u> very frightened.

The words underlined are words used when you write about something that is happening now.

● Write about something you imagine is happening now.

Getting you thinking

The writer was not happy with his work. He decided to write 'Eric and the Red Dragon' again. He wanted to write it as if it happened some time ago.

Example:

Eric <u>could</u> see the red dragon. It <u>was</u> ugly and big and scary. The red dragon <u>opened</u> its large mouth and <u>breathed</u> fire. The fire <u>was</u> coming straight towards him. Eric <u>was</u> very frightened.

How does it work?

The writer had to change **present** words into **past** words.

Present	Past
is	was
open	opened
breathe	breathed
can	could

Now you try it

Re-write the story below, changing it from the present to the past. The words you need to change have been underlined for you.

Hamish the Bold

Hamish is a bold man. He can see that the small fat thief is running away with the famous blue diamond. He is going to stop the thief. He is going to rescue the diamond.

Development activity

Form a tunnel. One of your group will walk through the tunnel and each person forming the tunnel will whisper a word from the past tense as the person walks through. The word should be about Hamish or the thief.

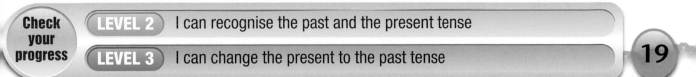

Getting you thinking

Short sentences can be joined together to make longer sentences. You can do this by adding **and**, **but**, **so** or **because**.

Example 1:

The bomb went off. Jemma was frightened.

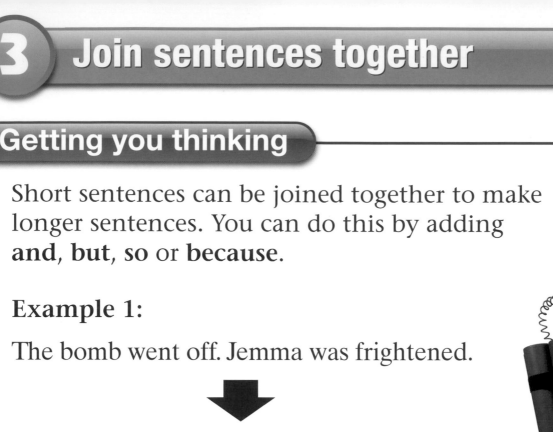

The bomb went off <u>and</u> Jemma was frightened.

Example 2:

A car skidded. The road was icy.

A car skidded <u>because</u> the road was icy.

How does it work?

By using joining words, you can turn two small sentences into one longer sentence. This can make your writing more interesting.

Now you try it

Join these sentences together with **and**, **but**, **so** or **because**.

a   Louise had a headache. She refused to take a tablet.

b   The day was hot. We went to the beach.

c   The forest fire was fierce. The firefighters put it out.

d   Amy liked music. She bought a new CD.

Development activity APP

Starting sentences in different ways

By changing the order of your sentences around you can make them more varied.

Examples:

1   If it snows, I might miss school.

2   I might miss school, if it snows.

○   Write four sentences about a storm at sea. Make them as varied as possible. Try to avoid always starting with 'It', 'I' or 'The storm'.

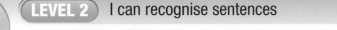

Level Booster

LEVEL 2

- I can vary my sentences
- I can recognise interesting sentences
- I can recognise the past and the present tense

LEVEL 3

- I can use the past and the present tense
- I can write interesting sentences
- I can join sentences together using **and**, **but**, **so** and **because**

LEVEL 4

- I can vary my sentence length
- I am usually accurate in my use of sentences
- I can vary the subject of my sentences

Chapter 3

AF4 Construct paragraphs and use cohesion within and between paragraphs

This chapter is going to show you how to

- Recognise paragraphs
- Use supporting sentences
- Arrange paragraphs.

What's it all about?

You will be able to use paragraphs correctly.

Getting you thinking

Remember sentences?

You know what a sentence is. It is a set of words making a complete statement. A sentence starts with a capital letter and usually ends with a full stop.

A paragraph is one or more sentences about one main idea or subject. Writers start a new paragraph to show readers that they are going to write about a new idea or subject.

Example:

Look at the five sentences below. They are all about one subject.

A grumpy old elf had a long red beard. He loved his long red beard. One day his long red beard caught fire. The long red beard started to burn. The grumpy old elf danced around the room as his beard burned.

How does it work?

The first sentence tells us the elf had a long red beard. The sentences that follow tell us more about the elf and his beard.

Now you try it

Have a look at the four sentences below.
See if you can work out which one is the most important sentence. It is sometimes called the **topic** sentence.

Jamie Duff needed glasses. He kicked a ball. But the ball was a hard, round stone! Jamie's toes hurt. His friends laughed.

Development activity APP

1 Sometimes, the most important sentence does not come first. See if you can work out which is the most important sentence here.

Teachers were frightened. Mice had invaded the school. They crawled onto the dinner plates. They chewed food in the kitchen. They crawled into the headteacher's hair.

2 Write four or five sentences about Mr Green, who saw mini-beasts invade his garden.

Check your progress

LEVEL 2   I can recognise a topic sentence

LEVEL 3   I can write five imaginative sentences

Getting you thinking

The other sentences in a paragraph are called supporting sentences.

A grumpy old elf had a long red beard. He loved his long red beard. One day his long red beard caught fire. The long red beard started to burn. — supporting sentences

How does it work?

The supporting sentences give us more detail about what is happening.

Now you try it

Look at the following paragraph. Copy out the sentences and underline the supporting sentences.

Angie wanted to be good at tennis. She practised every day. She hit the ball against a wall. She watched videos about her favourite players. Her younger sister still beat her.

Development activity APP

Pictures into paragraphs

- Working in pairs, try and work out what order the pictures go in.

- Now write a paragraph about what happens in the pictures. Try and use a sentence for each picture.

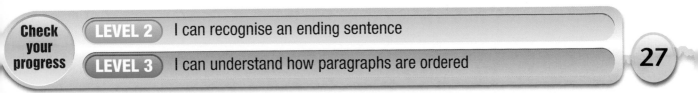

Getting you thinking

The story below is jumbled up. It is divided into four paragraphs but the paragraphs are mixed up.

Cousin Mike

a One day, I found a room full of really big hairy spiders. I took the spiders and put them in a box. I put the box through Cousin Mike's letterbox.

b If a child fell over in the park, Mike would laugh. If a child cried, he would laugh even more. If a child had a fever he would laugh until he cried.

c I heard Mike scream. He ran out of the house and down the road. Nobody saw him again.

d Cousin Mike was a horror. He hated spiders and he hated having a good time. He hated watching television. He hated watching sport. Most of all, he hated children.

● Working in pairs, see if you can work out the right order.

How does it work?

The paragraphs should be easy to sort because most stories follow a clear order.

Now you try it

Read 'Cousin Mike' again. Which is the topic sentence of each paragraph? What is each paragraph about?

Development activity APP

Here is a story about a shipwreck.

We had decided to sail across the Atlantic Ocean. We set off from New York. We wanted to reach the west coast of England. We were doing fine until a storm hit us. This was the worst storm we'd ever seen. The wind rocked our tiny boat. We decided to get below deck. We didn't want anyone swept overboard. A big wave flipped our boat over. We were trapped inside our cabin. We were upside down. It was getting difficult to breath. We didn't want to die.

This story is made of three paragraphs.

- Can you work out where each new paragraph should start?

- Complete the story about a shipwreck by writing a paragraph of your own.

| LEVEL 2 | I can sort paragraphs into a logical order |
| LEVEL 3 | I can write the final paragraph of a story |

Level Booster

LEVEL 2

- I can write using paragraphs
- I can recognise a topic sentence
- I can recognise an ending sentence

LEVEL 3

- I can write using supporting sentences within paragraphs
- I can write imaginative sentences
- I can recognise how paragraphs are ordered

LEVEL 4

- I can pick out the main point in a paragraph
- I can write in paragraphs
- I can support my main point with other sentences
- I can link ideas between paragraphs

Chapter 4

AF3 Organise and present whole texts effectively, sequencing and structuring information, ideas and events

This chapter is going to show you how to

- Use bullet points and headings
- Plan and make a speech.

What's it all about?

You will be able to organise your ideas.

Getting you thinking

You are going to find out all you can about some animals. When you have discovered some facts, you are going to write about them in a way that is easy to read.

Amazing Facts:

The Grey Squirrel

- Not all grey squirrels are grey. A few are black or red. Black squirrels have been spotted in parts of England.

- Grey squirrel babies are called kittens.

- Kittens are born with their eyes closed and without any teeth or hair.

- Grey squirrels can swim.

How does it work?

The writer has used a bullet point for each new fact about squirrels.

Now you try it

1 Use the internet or read library books to find out more about the animal or insect that interests you the most.

2 See if you can find four or five amazing facts. Set them out like the example, using bullet points for each new fact.

Development activity APP

Writing about your animal:

Find out as much information as you can about your chosen animal.

Now you have some information about your animal, you might want to set out a fact sheet using headings.

These might be

- Where it lives and hunts
- Home life
- Defence
- Description
- Problems
- Amazing facts
- Conclusion or ending.

If you set out your fact sheet using headings, it is easy for the reader to see what each section is about.

Wildcat fact sheet

See how the Wildcat fact sheet has been filled in.

Where wildcats live and hunt

Wildcats mostly live and hunt in Highland forests in Scotland. They usually hunt alone. They mark out their **territory** by leaving a scent. The male wildcat has **glands** on its feet. The glands are full of scent.

Home life

Wildcat kittens are born in a **den**. They leave the den when they are a month old. Their mother teaches them to hunt very soon after they are born.

Defence

Wildcats can growl and spit. They mock-charge, pretending they are lions!

Description

The wildcat looks like a strong tabby. Its coat is brown with black stripes or spots. Wildcats walk like lions and they have thick bushy tails.

Problems

People thought wildcats were pests so they were hunted and killed. There are now only four hundred wildcats left in Scotland.

Conclusion

Wildcats are interesting because they look like pet cats. But, they are different from pet cats and can never be tamed.

By setting the information out using headings, the reader can find information about the animal quickly. It is easier to read.

Glossary

territory: area the animal feels it owns

glands: part of the body that releases chemicals

den: an animal's home

- Set out your headings and write a few sentences underneath each heading.

  When you have finished, you will have a fact sheet about your favourite animal.

- Working in pairs, read each other's fact sheets and say how the fact sheets can be improved.

Getting you thinking

Sometimes in school you will need to give a speech. Before giving a speech, it is a good idea to have a plan. You can do this by making a flow chart. This will help you get your ideas in order.

Example:

Anita decided she wanted to speak about puppies and dogs. This is because she was given a puppy for her birthday. She's now training it. She is not an expert, but she knows something about the subject.

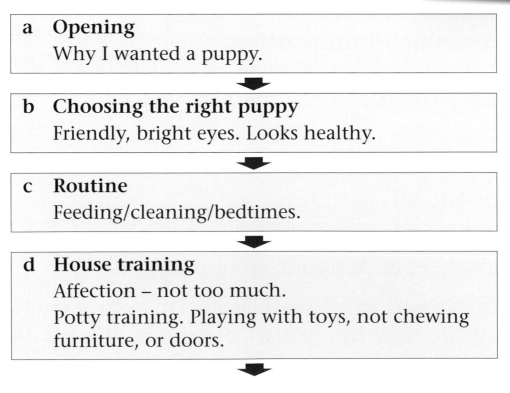

a Opening
Why I wanted a puppy.

b Choosing the right puppy
Friendly, bright eyes. Looks healthy.

c Routine
Feeding/cleaning/bedtimes.

d House training
Affection – not too much.
Potty training. Playing with toys, not chewing furniture, or doors.

e   Visiting the vet
Check health. Injections.

f   Puppy training
Walking on a lead. Acting properly around other dogs and people.

g   Problem dogs
Rescue dogs. Vicious dogs. How to cure bad behaviour.

How does it work?

If you have a good plan to use, you won't get stuck when you are talking.

Now you try it

Think of a subject you are interested in and you know something about. Find out more about it by using the library or the internet. Now set out headings, as Anita has done. Underneath the headings, write a sentence or two about that topic.

Development activity APP

Write and deliver your speech following the guidelines given.

Check your progress

| LEVEL 2 | I can write a plan for a speech |
| LEVEL 3 | I can write and give a speech |

Level Booster

LEVEL 2

- I can find out information and set it out correctly
- I can use bullet points
- I can write simple sentences under headings
- I can speak in front of my group

LEVEL 3

- I can write a fact sheet and set it out with bullet points
- I can research information
- I can write interesting information under headings
- I can make a plan
- I can write and deliver a speech

LEVEL 4

- I can write a clear opening and conclusion
- I can order my writing logically
- I can keep my writing organised
- I can use some linking words and phrases
- I can present my work effectively on the page

Chapter 5

AF1 Write imaginative, interesting and thoughtful texts

This chapter is going to show you how to
- Express opinions.

What's it all about?

You will be able to write about your views.

Getting you thinking

Viewpoint

Here are some people of your own age, giving their opinions about music.

Laura: I think N-Dubz is the best band because they started up from nothing. They are a hip-hop group from London and they sing about things that really matter.

Zoe: I think Leona Lewis is the best pop singer because she can really sing, not like some pop stars. 'I Will Be' is a fantastic song and she sings it really well.

Jordon: Alexandra Burke is a really powerful singer. I like what she's done with 'Hallelujah'. I really hope she goes on to sing many more songs.

How does it work?

Three students of your own age have told you who their favourite bands and singers are. They have told you why they like that particular band or singer.

Now you try it

What is your favourite band or singer?

Once you have picked a band or a singer to write about, you need to know what they have done. Write down a few pieces of information about the band or singer and give your views.

My favourite singer is / band are because...

Music Personality of the Year

Who do you think is the music personality of the year?

Example:

I think Alexandra Burke is the music personality of the year because she won X Factor singing some great songs.

You would write:

I think... is the music personality of the year because...

Grand Final

Each member of the class has voted for the music personality of the year. Add up the votes and list the three people who got the most votes.

1

2

3

Now vote for the best of the top three. Who has won? Who is the music personality of the year?

Development activity

Dream On Sports Personality of the Year

Read the extracts and decide who will be the sports personality of the year.

1 **Jim ('trip 'em up') Farell**

At last, a British marathon runner. Jim won the Chicago marathon in a record 2 hours 2 minutes. He aims to do well in the Olympics next year.

2 Dale ('take a dive') Jones

Nobody expected England to win the World Cup this year. That was before Dale Jones was selected to play centre forward. He scored a hat trick in the semi-final against Germany and another hat trick in the final.

3 Christina ('over the net') Drummond

The British tennis star that won Wimbledon is just fourteen years old. She beat both Williams sisters to reach the final and beat Maria Sharapova in the final by a staggering score of 6-1, 6-2. This is the first time any British tennis player has won a Wimbledon title for many years.

4 Don ('out for a duck') Steel

This amazing cricketer has broken all records in one season. He was put into bat against Australia, when the score was 0 for 3 wickets. He managed to reach a total of 316 not out and remind people that his nickname was a joke. He batted in the hot Australian sun for five long hours. England went on to win the match.

Level Booster

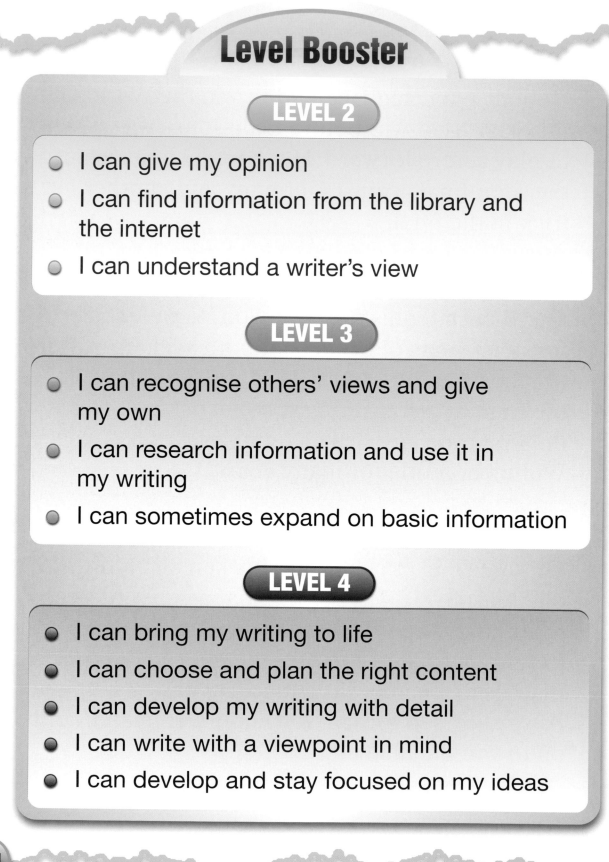

LEVEL 2

- I can give my opinion
- I can find information from the library and the internet
- I can understand a writer's view

LEVEL 3

- I can recognise others' views and give my own
- I can research information and use it in my writing
- I can sometimes expand on basic information

LEVEL 4

- I can bring my writing to life
- I can choose and plan the right content
- I can develop my writing with detail
- I can write with a viewpoint in mind
- I can develop and stay focused on my ideas

Chapter 6

AF7 Select appropriate and effective vocabulary

This chapter is going to show you how to

- Choose interesting verbs
- Write using adjectives.

What's it all about?

You will be able to improve your vocabulary.

Getting you thinking

A verb is a doing or being word.

Examples: I am, she runs

How does it work?

If you did not use verbs, a piece of writing would not make sense.

I (went) to the cinema. I was late so I (ran) all the way there. My friend was late because he (went) for a swim and forgot the time.

Now you try it

Look at the following piece of writing. The verbs are missing. Put the right verbs in the right place.

Yesterday, the sun _____. I _____ for a picnic. I _____ my food and _____ my drink. As soon as lunch was over I _____ home.

slurped	gobbled	walked	went	shone

Development activity

Some verbs are more interesting than others.

Replace the verbs underlined with different verbs of your own choice.

It was sports day. I tried the high jump and ran around the track. I walked to the refreshment tent and bought a drink. I then purchased some sandwiches.

Getting you thinking

Adjectives can make your description more lively.

Example:

Monday was a dull day. Mum drove me to school in our car. Mr Fothergill was waiting for me. He looked angry. I wasn't wearing the school uniform. I was still dressed in my pyjamas.

If adjectives were added, this would read:

Monday was a dark dull day. Mum drove me to school in our bright blue sports car. Red-faced Mr Fothergill was waiting for me. He looked very angry. I wasn't wearing the deep yellow school uniform. I was still dressed in my old striped pyjamas.

How does it work?

Using adjectives can make your work much more interesting.

Now you try it

Mrs Wheeler was wearing her _____ coat. It was a _____ day but she still wore the _____ coat. Her husband wore a _____ even on _____ days.

If you get stuck, here is a bank of words you could use.

> old, thick, brown, glorious, crisp, warm, vest, frosty, stringy

Development activity APP

Vocabulary

It is interesting to try new words in your writing. Using new words will make your writing more adventurous.

Can you think of an adjective to describe each of these people or things?

1 dog   4 baby
2 car   5 witch
3 teacher   6 axe

Now write a sentence for each of the words, using your adjectives.

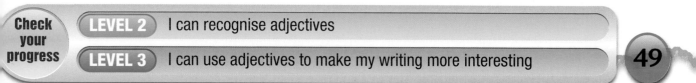

Check your progress

LEVEL 2 I can recognise adjectives

LEVEL 3 I can use adjectives to make my writing more interesting

Level Booster

LEVEL 2

- I can recognise verbs in a sentence
- I can recognise adjectives in a sentence

LEVEL 3

- I can think about the words I choose when writing
- I can use adjectives to improve my choice of words

LEVEL 4

- I can generally use interesting vocabulary
- I can expand my vocabulary to match a chosen topic
- I can use adjectives and adverbs to add detail to my writing

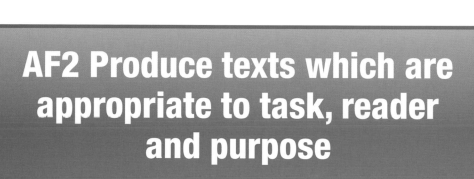

Chapter 7

AF2 Produce texts which are appropriate to task, reader and purpose

This chapter is going to show you how to

- Recognise and write an exciting story opening
- Write an exciting middle and end.

What's it all about?

You will be able to recognise and write an interesting story.

Getting you thinking

Read the three story openings below and decide which one you like the best.

Example A: Spook Manor.

No one can live for long in Spook Manor. Many people have tried, but most of them ended up crazy, or dead – and I mean really, really dead! But somewhere hidden in Spook Manor there is a great treasure, an ancient painting worth millions! Who is brave enough to search for it?

Example B: Dark Detective.

Scotland Yard is the famous address of London's police: it is known all over the world for cracking crime and solving mysteries. But it has a secret – a big, dark, nasty secret.

In a gloomy office you will find a man with a long, dark overcoat. If you ask his name, he'll smile like a skull and say: 'I'm Detective Max Darke, Demon Division'.

Example C: The Old Sweet Shop.

The old sweet shop at the corner of the street had been shut for years. One day it opened again. An old lady served behind the counter. Behind her, on the walls, were long wooden shelves. The shelves were filled with jars of sweets.

When children entered the shop, the old lady appeared. She did not speak to anyone. She just nodded when someone ordered sweets. Some said she was a ghost. But she was **not** a ghost – she was something **far scarier**!

Now you try it

Plan the start of a story by writing down at least four good ideas. Think of a good title. List three or four ideas that might happen in the first few sentences.

- Now write the start of your story, using about seven sentences.

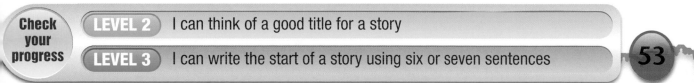

Getting you thinking

If the middle of a story is boring, readers might lose interest.

Try to make the middle of your story as exciting as the start.

Example:

Read 'The Old Sweet Shop' again. This is what happens later on in the story.

1   The old lady's face sometimes changes.

2   The face seems to become an alien's face.

3   The lady serves two children and her body begins to change.

The middle of the story

Suzi and Rory were shocked. The old lady was changing into a green alien. The sweets in her hand looked like poison. Rory suddenly realised that the aliens were poisoning everyone. They wanted people to be too ill to stop an alien invasion.

How does it work?

The writer makes the middle interesting by giving the reader some new information.

We now know the old lady is an alien and that aliens are about to invade Earth!

We hope that Rory and Suzi can do something about it!

Now you try it

Take 'Spook Manor' or 'Dark Detective' and think of some ideas for the middle of the story.

Development activity APP

1 **Leading up to an interesting end**

The end needs to be exciting. In 'The Old Sweet Shop', what can be done to make the end exciting? Look at what might lead up to that exciting end.

Example:

1 Rory and Suzi tell grown-ups about the invasion. Nobody believes them.

2 Rory and Suzi sneak into the shop at night

3 Twenty aliens are sitting around a table, looking at a map of the world.

4 Rory sends a text message to the army. Suzi and Rory are spotted by the aliens and chased.

The writer has planned exciting new ideas to keep us interested and to lead on to the amazing ending.

- Think about interesting or exciting things that could happen in your story.

- Number the ideas 1–4. They **should** lead to an amazing ending!

2   The End

Example:

> Rory and Suzi were trapped in the sweet shop. They were cornered. They knew they were about to die.
>
>
>
> An alien grinned. He was the leader. He was going to kill them himself.
>
> There was a loud crash as the door was smashed. The army had arrived. Gunshots were fired. The aliens were taken by surprise. The leader turned, too late. A bullet hit his chest. He groaned and fell, dead! Some aliens were killed. Some were captured. Rory and Suzi had saved planet Earth. They were heroes.

The writer made the story exciting until the very end. There was no chance of the reader getting bored.

- See if you can come up with an exciting end for your story. Use about five or six sentences to end your story.

Level Booster

- I can think of a good title for a story
- I can plan and write an interesting start to a story
- I can plan a good middle for a story
- I can plan a good ending for a story

LEVEL 3

- I can write an interesting start to a story
- I can write using six or seven sentences
- I can sustain a story by making the middle interesting
- I can end a story, keeping it exciting

LEVEL 4

- I can decide what kind of writing I am being asked to do
- I can include some of the features of a type of writing
- I can write in the correct style for the task
- I can develop a clear viewpoint in my writing

Chapter 8

AF8 Use correct spelling

This chapter is going to show you how to
- Recognise similar sounding words
- Learn spellings.

What's it all about?

You will learn new ideas to improve your spelling.

Getting you thinking

Example:

fair   fare

Both these words sound the same but they mean different things.

I'm riding on the dodgems at the <u>fair</u>.

I paid my bus <u>fare</u> today.

How does it work?

Some words sound the same but they are spelt in a different way.

Now you try it

Copy the sentences into your books and cross out what you think is the wrong spelling. After you have done the exercise, check with your teacher.

1   I saw an angel/angle and it had wings.

2   I blew/blue on the fire.

3   The pop banned/band played in the Town Hall.

4   My brother lost his pear/pair of socks.

5 I could cell/sell my mobile phone.

6 My mum got some bargains in the January sale/sail.

7 I could tie that knot/not.

8 Rebecca ate/eight her dinner after ate/eight.

Development activity

Poetry spelling

Each line in the poem below needs an ending.

The Sailor
There once was a ....
Who needed a ....
He slipped on the ....
As he walked in the ....
Made an ....
In his ....
Which meant the.........
Came out a ....

Complete the poem by filling in the missing words.

| error, door, tailor, terror, major, sailor, sailor, floor |

Getting you thinking

Look – 'Think' – Say – Cover – Write – Check

You should keep a spelling book. When you have made a mistake write the correct spelling of the word in your book.

You can learn how to spell the word by using the following method:

1 **Look** at the word very carefully.

2 **Think** about the parts of the word that might cause problems.

3 **Say** the word out loud or in your head.

4 **Cover** the word up.

5 **Write** the word out without looking at it again

6 **Check** to see if you have got it right

If you have still misspelt the word, follow 1–6 again.

How does it work?

If you keep looking at the correct spelling and use the **look – 'think' – say – cover – write – check** method, you should learn to spell the word correctly.

Now you try it APP

Here are some spellings. Working in pairs, try spelling these words and get your partner to test you and check them.

You have already met these words in this chapter.

1. sailor
2. fair
3. banned
4. following
5. correct
6. spelling
7. sentence
8. knot
9. brother
10. burst

Write out any words you did not get right and use the **look – 'think' – say – cover – write – check** method. Then retest yourself.

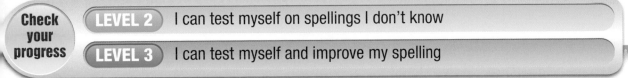

Check your progress

LEVEL 2 I can test myself on spellings I don't know

LEVEL 3 I can test myself and improve my spelling

Level Booster

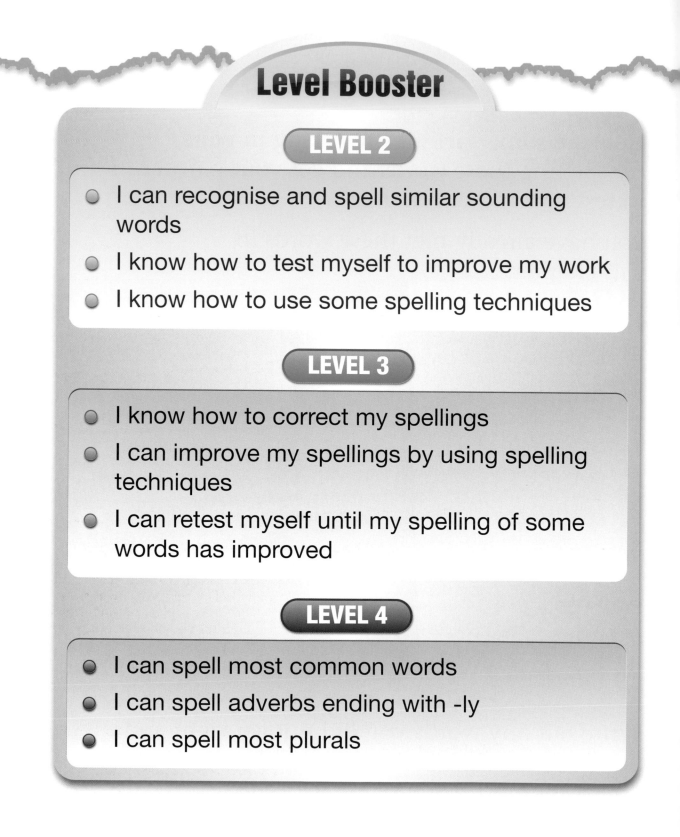

LEVEL 2

- I can recognise and spell similar sounding words
- I know how to test myself to improve my work
- I know how to use some spelling techniques

LEVEL 3

- I know how to correct my spellings
- I can improve my spellings by using spelling techniques
- I can retest myself until my spelling of some words has improved

LEVEL 4

- I can spell most common words
- I can spell adverbs ending with -ly
- I can spell most plurals

Teacher Guide

Where the final task of the double-page section is substantial enough to provide a snapshot of students' progress, this has been marked as an **APP opportunity**.

Each double-page section ends with a **Check your progress** box. This offers a levelled checklist against which students can self- or peer-assess their final piece of writing from the **Development** or **Now you try it** section.

The end of chapter **Level Booster** is a less task-specific checklist of the skills students need to master to reach Level 2, 3 and 4. It can be used to help students see the level they are working at currently and to visualise what they need to do to make progress.

This book acknowledges the fact that students aiming for Level 3 will perform better if they are given starter activities that relate to the work they need to learn. The activities will appeal to students with different learning styles

Chapter 1 AF6 Write with technical accuracy of syntax and punctuation in phrases, sentences and clauses

STARTER 1

Making sentences: Sentence Game

The sun shines on...

Place chairs in a circle. Choose one person to stand in the middle.
The rest of the group will need to sit on their chairs.
Take the spare chair away.

The person in the middle calls 'The sun shines on …'
A student (selected if you wish) completes the sentence.

An example might be: 'The sun shines on all those who have a pet cat.'
Tell students that this is a sentence; it is a sentence because it makes sense.

Students who own a pet cat will need to change places with somebody else who owns a pet cat. There is one rule: the student cannot change places with the student who sits next to him/her.

The caller will try and find a seat. The student who does not have a seat is the next caller.

Once students get into the game they should produce examples such as:

The sun shines on everyone who supports Liverpool.

The sun shines on everyone wearing a watch.

The sun shines on everyone whose first name starts with the letter 'P'.

Unfortunately/fortunately

This is another game to reinforce understanding of what makes a sentence. Keeping students sitting in the circle, get them to take it in turns to say a sentence and build up a story.

Examples:

'Unfortunately, Lee fell into the sea.'

'Fortunately, he could swim.'

'Unfortunately, there were sharks in the water.'

'Fortunately, there was a boat near by.'

(Allow the students to carry on going round the circle for as long as they can. If they get stuck, start a new round.)

STARTER 3

'Master, master – who am I?'

You will need space for this game.

Select one student to be blindfolded and placed carefully on a chair.

Ask another student to disguise their voice and approach the blindfolded person. The selected

student says, 'Master, master – who am I?'

The blindfolded student must guess, and speak using a sentence. They should say something like:

'I think you are Suzie', or 'You sound like Joe'.

STARTER 4

To reinforce the use of capital letters and full stops, play the 'clap/click' game. Students are asked to clap hands for a capital letter and click their fingers when there should be a full stop. Use the 'The sun shines on …' examples and the 'fortunately/unfortunately' examples or the sentences below.

Lewis Hamilton is a champion.

Some footballers miss open goals.

My mates hang out down town.

I'm having a sleepover this weekend.

We're going to Spain this summer.

I have a naughty new puppy.

A variation of the clap/click game can be as follows:

Students clap hands for a capital letter and click their fingers for a full stop. They can stamp one foot for a question mark and both feet for an exclamation mark. (Teachers beware: the game may be noisy and effective!)

Here are some ideas:

Do you think it will snow today? (stamp one foot)

Hey! You! (stamp both feet)

Stop at once! (stamp both feet)

Have you seen the wolf? (stamp one foot)

1 Recognise a sentence

Getting you thinking

Read the two sentences to students. If students require more practice, here are two more sentences:

A rat bit Lady Glamour.

James Winters loved hot summer days.

How does it work?

Students can try these sentences for more practice.

Mr Driver… his car. Oliver Newman… his dad's car.

Ask students how many words they can think of to make the sentences correct.

Write the words on the board.

Now you try it

You might want to photocopy this page rather than get students to copy it into their books.

66

2 Use capital letters

Getting you thinking

Show students a range of sentences that begin with capital letters. Here are three examples:

1) The show must go on. 2) My auntie gave me fifty pounds. 3) The best team won.

How does it work?

Explain to students that without capital letters it is hard to understand what is being written.

Now you try it

Explain to students that the capital letters in this example are all used at the start of a sentence.

Development

Explain to students that the first sentence needs one capital letter, the second needs three, the third needs two and the fourth needs two. The fifth needs three and the sixth needs three. Can they work out why and where?

3 Use full stops, exclamation marks and question marks

Getting you thinking

Explain that questions and exclamations are spoken in different ways. For example, if you were asking, 'Are you mad?', your voice might rise at the end of the sentence but if you were shouting, 'Come here now!', your voice might sound harsh throughout.

Explain that most sentences end in a full stop.

Explain that students can work out where full stops go by the fact that the capital letter shows a new sentence is about to start.

Now you try it

Sentence 1 is not a question. It is a command. A games teacher or somebody in the army could have spoken it loudly. It needs an exclamation mark.

Look sharp, lad!

Sentence 2 is a question, so it will need a question mark.

How many cats have you got?

Sentence 3 is not a question and it does not need an exclamation mark. It is a statement, so it just needs a full stop.

I've lost my homework.

Development

You may want to try more examples with students before moving on to the six sentences.

Model the first sentence as an example.

4 Recognise speech in stories

Getting you thinking

Model the story by reading it to the group.

How does it work?

Get a member of the class to speak. Write what is said on the board. Allow students to place speech marks around the words that are actually spoken.

Now you try it

Model the first sentence for the students. You may wish to photocopy the four sentences that need speech marks.

STARTER 1

The Mime Game

Students need to sit on chairs and mime the action:

1 Imagine you are sitting on a chair in a restaurant.

They will need to mime the action. They might mime eating, talking, drinking, rubbing their full tummies, etc. Allow the best at miming to illustrate a good example to others.

2 Imagine that you are babies, sitting in highchairs.

They will possibly mime shaking a rattle, being fed, pounding fists, playing with a toy, sucking a dummy, etc.

3 Imagine that you are sitting in a dentist's chair, the chair on a plane, a boat or a car.

This time, the rest of the group need to guess where they are.

4 They no longer mime the action, but talk … as if it is all in the present.

When the talking is finished, ask students to say a sentence as if their mime was in the past.

You could give students the following examples:

'Last week I ate in a restaurant.'

'I went to the dentist yesterday.'

'Once, a long time ago, I was a baby sitting in a highchair.'

STARTER 2

The Past/Present Game

Ask students to think of something that happened in the past. They can say out loud what happened. Possible examples:

'I went on holiday to America.' 'My baby brother was born.' 'I had an accident.'

Point out that *went*, *was* and *had* are all words we use when talking about the past.

Ask them to think of something that is happening now. (Avoid the future.)

'We are in an English lesson.' 'We are listening to the teacher.' ' My friend isn't listening.'

Explain that the words *are* and *isn't*, are words we have just used when talking about what is happening now.

1 Recognise the present and the past tense in stories

Getting you thinking

Read the story to the students. Go through the story with them, pointing out features that show it was written in the past.

Now you try it

Students might want to think about something that has happened in their past. Teachers could suggest an amusing incident or something that sticks out in their mind, such as a special holiday or event.

If students are still stuck, they could use a writing frame. Perhaps suggest a visit to the fair or the zoo?

Suggested past tense writing frame

Some time ago I went…
At the funfair I went on…
After the rides, I…
Then…
For my lunch I ate…
A funny thing happened when…
What I remember best is…

Suggested present tense writing frame

We arrive at the zoo
We arrive by…
We're looking at the…
Now we're looking at the… They have…   and they…
We're at the reptile house. I like the…best.
We're eating… My sandwiches are…

Now we're back…
I really enjoyed…
The best part was…

2 Turn the present into the past

Getting you thinking

Explain to students that the words underlined have been changed from the original, so that the story is told as if it had happened in the past.

Now you try it

You might allow students to change all the underlined words from 'Hamish the Bold' into the past tense before they rewrite the passage.

3 Join sentences together

Getting you thinking

As a starter, you could ask students to change the examples by using other joining words.

Examples:

The bomb went off **so** Jemma was frightened.

A car skidded **when** the road was icy.

Now you try it

You may wish to photocopy this exercise.

Students can practise this exercise orally before they write.

Development

Explain that they only need to use about five or six sentences in their own piece of writing.

When students have completed this exercise, allow them to read their work to the rest of the group. See how many variations there are.

Development

The tunnel is a variation of a thought tunnel. Students line up in two rows facing each other to form a tunnel. Students whispering words from the present tense, in a second round, can extend the game.

Development

When students have written their sentences about a storm at sea, allow them to rewrite the sentences by changing the sentence around or offering a different variation in some way. Get the class to vote on which variation they prefer.

If possible, allow students to use their IT skills and write the sentences on a word processor.

Chapter 3 AF4 Construct paragraphs and use cohesion between paragraphs

STARTER 1

Making Paragraphs. The Paragraph Game

A variation of 'The sun shines on…' is 'The rain pours on… because…'

This time, sentences need to follow one another, to form a paragraph.

Place chairs in a circle. Students sit on chairs and the teacher sits in the middle of the circle.

Begin the game and choose a student to continue. The game continues clockwise.

Example:

Teacher: The rain pours on mean old Mr Cross.

Student 1: Because he keeps his money to himself.

Student 2: He never spends and he always saves.

Student 3: He's like Scrooge, the mean old man.

Once the group get the idea of the game, you could always do without 'The rain pours on… and encourage students to link sentences together.

Example:
You: An alien arrived at school one day.
Student 1: It had small eyes and a green skin.
Student 2: It came into our classroom.
Student 3: We hid under our desks.

Should student interest begin to fade, clap to end the round and start a new one.

After the games, explain to students that they have all made up a story on the same topic. They have linked their sentences together. If they wrote down all the sentences they had said, they would have made a paragraph.

STARTER 2

'I went shopping…' is a variation of the memory game, '…and in my bag I put …'

Students should sit in a circle. Start the activity by saying, 'I went shopping and in my bag I put… a cabbage.'

1 Choose a student to place another item in the bag, and so on.

2 After about six or seven items are in the bag, and to extend the game, tell them the bag has split and all the shopping has fallen out!

Example:
'My bag split and out fell… a packet of tea, a loaf of bread, a cabbage…'

Students need to remember and recite the shopping list in reverse!

3 Then tell students that the shopkeeper has given you a new bag. They will now need to place the items into the new bag, and recite the original order.

4 Finally, tell them you have arrived home and you need to unpack the shopping. Again, the last item becomes the first one out.

1 Recognise Paragraphs

Getting you thinking

This is a revision exercise to re-enforce students' understanding of sentences and to introduce paragraphs as groups of sentences.

How does it work?

Explain to students that the first – or most important sentence – is known as the **topic sentence**.

Now you try it

Explain to students that the first sentence is the topic sentence as it explains why the stone was mistaken for a ball.

Development

a Explain to students that the topic sentence is the second one. The other sentences tell us where the mice had invaded and how people feel about them!

b This exercise will test whether students can write a topic and supporting sentences.

2 Use supporting sentences

Getting you thinking

You may wish to show students supporting sentences, using examples from other stories.

How does it work?

Explain that topic sentences give students a clue as to what the paragraph will be about. The supporting sentences tell students more about the topic of the paragraph.

Now you try it

Students should underline all the sentences except the first one.

Development

For the two exercises, students should be able to work out the picture order. If not, allow student pairs to merge and talk about the order.

After the work on this topic, ask students to write a paragraph about somebody who has had a minor accident. Students can swap books with a partner and highlight the different sentences in different colour pens/highlighters. Students will need three different colour pens/highlighters for this activity.

3 Arrange paragraphs

Getting you thinking

Students should work out that the order is d,b,a,c.

You may wish to photocopy the paragraphs about Cousin Mike and allow students to cut them out and place them in a logical order.

Development

If you wish to develop the student's ability to write in paragraphs further, try this exercise. The story about the shipwreck is unfinished. Allow students to finish the story by adding a paragraph of their own.

Ask students to imagine what happened next. Get them to explore ideas orally before they write.

Ask students to describe (orally) what each sentence will be about, making sure they understand the story before they write their paragraph.

If you feel students need to understand the story before writing, get each to storyboard the four paragraphs about Cousin Mike, then they can storyboard their own.

IT Skills

Allow students to write their story using a word processing program. This will enable them to present their work neatly for a wall display.

The work that requires students to rearrange paragraphs (Cousin Mike) can also be word processed so that students have the opportunity to edit and rearrange text.

Chapter 4 AF3 Organise and present whole texts effectively, sequencing and structuring information, ideas and events

STARTER 1

Order. Can you do this?

Sitting at their desks, tell students to hold their left hand in the air pointing their fingers forward and drawing a circle in the air. They then drop their left hand, raise their right hand and draw a cross in the air. Then ask them to do the two things at the same time! Teachers beware: the game may be noisy and effective!

STARTER 2

This game shows students that it's easier to do one thing at a time.

The Alphabet Game

Around the class, ask students to think of something to go with each letter of the alphabet. If students are unsure of the alphabetical order, recite this to them.

You might get:

  A is for apple. B is for ball. C is for cat…

For a variation of the game, ask students to do the whole exercise again, backwards!

Teachers beware: this is a difficult exercise.

Point out to students that most things have a logical order.

The Order Game:

See how quickly students can put these words in order:

> change zoo game harp tank sail whale apple dark ball

Now they can try a more difficult order:

> crate cat bat bone bend clot break ball bank bit.

1 Use bullet points and headings

Getting you thinking

Students may know facts about squirrels and other animals. Allow them to talk about animals for a set period of time. Perhaps for five minutes?

How does it work?

Tell students this fact sheet works because the facts are presented in a logical order.

Using bullet points allows the reader to read the facts more easily. The reader will take in the new information, without being confused.

Students have had the Squirrel fact sheet. If you want to test the students' understanding of the fact sheet before you move on to allow them to make their own fact sheet, try them on these questions – responses may be oral or written. Students should be encouraged to answer using full sentences. Example: *Black squirrels have been seen in England.*

The Squirrel:

1 Where have black squirrels been seen?

2 Are squirrel kittens born with their eyes open?

3 What are squirrel kittens born without?

4 Can grey squirrels swim?

Now you try it

Students may need to be shown where they can find the required information. Take them to the library and show them the non-fiction section. Alternatively, bring a selection of relevant books to class.

Development

If students need another example of a fact sheet, give them this one on the wildcat.

After using the wildcat fact sheet

You might want to make sure students have understood the fact sheet. Again, this work below could be written or spoken.

Knowing about wildcats:

1 Where do wildcats live?

2 Do wildcats hunt in groups?

3 What does the male wildcat have on its feet?

4 Where are wildcat kittens born?

5 How do wildcats defend themselves?

6 What do wildcats look like?

7 Why are so few wildcats left in the wild?

2 Plan and make a speech

Getting you thinking

Show students what a flowchart is by showing them how the example works.

How does it work?

Show students Anita's plan and explain that they need a similar plan.

Allow students to bullet point ideas before they write a flow chart.

Now you try it

Explain to students that they need to write about something they know well.

Explain that they need to research the subject further, as Anita did. Help them to find appropriate books in the library, or bring in a selection to class.

Development

Drafting your speech

If you would like your students to go further with their speeches, you could give them this example:

Opening

Anita decided upon a quick opening, so that she could get into her subject without boring her classmates.

> *I had always wanted a puppy but mum said it would chew everything. She also wanted to know who'd take it for walks. I told her that she need not worry. I'd use my paper round money to get a puppy properly trained.*

Anita has explained how she overcame her mum's worries and persuaded her mum that she could look after a puppy. She is now ready to go on to the next part of her speech.

Write down the opening for your speech and try it out with a partner. Ask your partner to suggest ideas to improve your opening.

In groups, pick a number over one but under thirteen. Roll two dice. If your number comes up, it is your turn to speak. If two of you have the same number, roll the dice again, to see who speaks first!

Chapter 5 AF1 Write imaginative interesting and thoughtful texts

STARTER 1

To build up students' vocabulary and concentration, play the random word game. All you need for this is a children's fiction book. Ask students for a number from 1-100. Turn to that page. Now ask for a number from 1-30. This gives you the line. Now ask for a number from 1-10. This gives you the word. Write the selected word on the board. See if anyone can define it. (Teacher discretion is needed if the selected word is too easy or too hard.)

Play the game a few times until you have six words. See if the students can make a sentence using the six words. They can add pronouns and joining words if necessary.

If students find the exercise a struggle, choose your own six words.

Example:

seaside   holiday   we   near   are   on   the

This becomes: 'We are on holiday near the seaside.' Or: 'We are near the seaside, on holiday.'

STARTER 2

Working in pairs, students can play the Roll the Dice Game – avoiding sharks!

Students roll the dice and land on a square writing a word of their choice in the square. If they land on a shark square, they have to start again, with new words in the boxes. Once they complete a row, they have to make a sentence, adding joining words if necessary.

Example: Starting board

1 Empty box

	(Shark)				

2 Students written in above box.

Zoo	(Shark)	Went	I	the	to

Sentence: I went to the zoo.

Remember: If students use words that do not easily form sentences, they can use joining words.

1 Express opinions

Getting you thinking

Allow students to express their opinions concerning pop stars and bands. They may want to express opinions about the choices students of their own age have made.

How does it work?

Students should look in magazines or the internet and find more information about the singer or band they are to talk about.

Now you try it

In groups, students may want to present a small talk to the group.

Music Personality of the Year: Grand final

Allow students to write down their choices and narrow the final down to the top three choices. Then, allow them to vote for the overall winner.

Point out that they have expressed an opinion. Other classes/groups may not agree with them. Going further, ask them to write down which band they think is the best ever, giving reasons for their choices.

Grand final. Count up the votes yourself. Make the outcome as tense and exciting as possible.

Development

Students might need a writing frame for this activity.

Suggested writing frame

My favourite sports personality is...
(s)he played against...on Saturday.
... were lucky to...
My sports star played...
...scored a... when....
My player's team is... in the league but they could finish the season... if they play...

(Students will need to adapt the words, depending upon the sport or team their personality is involved in.)

Player writing frame

My favourite player is...
(S)he played against... recently.
... was lucky to....
My player played... and scored a... when...
(S)he is... in the world rankings but could... if (s)he plays...

(Teacher to adapt depending upon the sport chosen.)

Things students might also enjoy:

a   Vote for the person they think ought to be 'Dream On Sports Personality of the Year'.

b   Write their own 'Dream On Sports Personality'.

c   Read out their sports personality and allow the class to vote. The winner is the personality who receives the most votes.

Chapter 6 AF7 Select appropriate and effective vocabulary

STARTER 1

The memory and speaking game

These starter activities are designed to improve students' vocabulary.

Charades: Round One

Students write the name of a famous person on card or paper. They fold the paper and place it in a hat, or your empty bin. Each student must have one name in the hat. Names can be from the past or present. Examples could be famous pop stars, sports personalities or actors.

Students are then divided into two groups – group A and group B. One member from group A takes a name from the hat. That student then has to say what the person does, and say something about that person until a member of group A guesses who that person is. This exercise should stretch their vocabulary. Group A have one minute. If guessed correctly, group A hold that paper.

If not guessed, group B have one minute to guess correctly. Then group B have a turn to go first!

After Round One, A and B add up the cards they hold and their score is written down.

Charades: Round 2

The cards go back into the hat. One member from group A takes a name from the hat. That student mimes what the chosen person does. If students from group A guess correctly, A holds the card. They have one minute. If they have not guessed correctly, within the time limit, the card goes to group B.

Students do know, from Round One, who is on the cards – but can they remember?

The winning team is the one who holds the most cards. The overall team winners are those who have the most points over the two rounds.

STARTER 2

What do you know about me? A vocabulary stretching exercise.

Each student will need to write five things about themselves. Students should try and use words to describe something about themselves accurately. After they have secretly completed this writing, they will need to sit on chairs in a circle. They then mention one thing about themselves, until all in the group have had a turn.

They do this until the circle has been completed five times – so that each student has mentioned five things about themselves.

The teacher then chooses two students and one student is asked what he/she knows about the other student. They then swap roles. Which student has remembered the most about the other?

A further variation on this theme has students writing five things about themselves, but some are false. When a student is picked to say what he/she knows about the other, the other student can say 'true' or 'false.'

STARTER 3

The Police/Suspect Game

In this game, two to four students are suspected of committing a crime – it could be robbery or murder. They go to the corner of the room and work out an alibi, thinking about where they were for two hours, when the crime took place. The rest of the group are the police.

The police can ask the group any questions they like about the crime. They can ask individuals one at a time, if they wish. If the group alibis

tally, then the group are free. If not, they are accused of the crime.

Example:

The group need to work out where they were from 7pm in the evening until 9pm. They might decide they were at a restaurant at 7pm, they walked home and played on their computers until 8pm and went to play at the local arcade at 9pm.

1 Choose interesting verbs

Getting you thinking

Explain what a verb is in more detail to your students if you feel they need extra help.

How does it work?

Explain that 'went' and 'ran' are doing words.

Now you try it

The verbs 'slumped', 'gobbled', 'walked,' 'went' and 'shone' can be used to fill the gaps. Students can use their own verbs if they prefer.

Development

If students are stuck, you could supply the following words for them – did, walked, ran, took, stole.

2 Write using adjectives

Getting you thinking

Students need to realise that adjectives are important and their use can move students' work up a level.

How does it work?

Students should look at the examples with care and point out the adjectives.

Now you try it

Students should use the word bank if they are stuck.

Development

Students could keep a book as a word bank, to write in unfamiliar words and their meanings.

Chapter 7 AF2 Select texts which are appropriate to task reader and purpose

These activities are designed to help students learn about the structure of stories and how to keep a reader or listener interested.

STARTER 1

Catch a Story

The class will need a ball or a beanbag. They will need to sit in a circle. You start a story and throw the beanbag. The student who catches the beanbag will continue the story. Those who are shy or nervous may not catch the beanbag to join in. If you want everyone to participate, tell the group that they cannot catch the beanbag twice.

Part of this exercise is to allow students to make up exciting stories orally.

Example:

You: A wolf was seen heading for our school.
Laura: The wolf howled at the back door.
Elliott: We were scared it might get in.
Kermal: It had sharp claws and big yellow teeth.

If you feel the story is stagnating, end it and start a new one.

STARTER 2

Something Different: Observation

Place chairs in a circle. Allow students to observe one another. A volunteer leaves the room. Out of the room, the volunteer changes something about themselves. Perhaps the student might change his/her hairstyle, take a tie off, undo shoelaces or exchange shoes for trainers.

When the volunteer is back, students have to spot the difference. The student who spots the difference first, has a go at being different.

Explain to students that to write well, they need to be observant.

1 Recognise and write an exciting story opening

Getting you thinking

Model the three stories by reading each to students. Allow volunteers to read the stories after you have read them. Ideally, use three volunteers.

2) Students can make a storyboard of the story they like best. Again, it is the start of the story they should concentrate on.

Students can divide a plain sheet with three sections and draw the action. For example, in 'Dark Detective', they could start with the drawing of a police badge or the sign for Scotland Yard. The second drawing could be of detective Max Darke, in his sinister long overcoat. The third drawing could be of Max, grinning – skull-like.

Drawing the story can help students imagine what is happening in the story.

How does it work?

The three story openings all contain a mystery. The stories intrigue the reader and make the reader want to know more. The writer wants to make the start of the story as exciting as possible, so you can't put the book down! To do this, the writer will think of a really good idea and plan the start.

Now you try it

Allow students to think of their senses – hearing, sight, sound, touch and smell.

Ask them to think about how they could use each sense in their plan.

Explain to students that they should stick to their plan when they write their stories.

Development

After students have looked at 'Spook Manor,' 'Dark Detective,' and 'The Old Sweet Shop' they could freeze-frame a dramatic point in the story that they like best. 'Freeze-framing' is when students take a point in the story and freeze the action, as if a photograph has been taken.

If possible, students can act out what happens in the story up to the point of the freeze-frame.

Remember, it is the beginning of one of the three stories they are freeze-framing.

2 Write an exciting middle and end

Getting you thinking

Ask students to think of other ideas for 'The Old Sweet Shop'. Could they think of three alternative ideas? This will help them to think about how stories are formed.

How does it work?

Students may wish to compare their ideas to those of the writer. Which idea did they like the best and why?

Now you try it

Before writing the story, students might like to draw a storyboard for the middle of their chosen story. If they have chosen 'Dark Detective', they might want to divide their drawing paper into six sections – one for each section.

The first could be – Max discovers somebody has been murdered.

The second – He suspects a shape shifter has murdered somebody.

The third – He has a tip-off that leads him to a hotel.

The fourth – He has trouble getting into the hotel. The porter thinks he's dirty and looks evil.

The fifth – Max is in the hallway. He notices the man's skin colour is changing.

The sixth – The man is shape shifting into something else!

Underneath the drawings, students could describe the action in one sentence.

Development

Again, using the storyboard idea, students can divide their paper into six – using one drawing for each sentence they intend to write.

Some ideas for students who are stuck:

The first – Max tries to arrest the shape shifter.

The second – suddenly, a master shape shifter appears.

The third – this creature has claws instead of hands. Its teeth are large.

The fourth – this creature has its claws around Max's throat.

The fifth – Max has an assistant, Cloe. She arrives just in time and her secret formula, garlic, overpowers the evil creature.

The sixth – Max and Cloe handcuff the evil creature.

Note: The task is to get students drawing, using their imaginations.

Once the students have completed their storyboarding, they can act out the stories in small groups. They should then write the stories into their books, before reading their stories to another group. Ask them which story they liked best and why.

Read the real stories, *Dark Detective* by Jane West and *Spook Manor* by David Orme, both Badger Publishing.

STARTER 1

Hangman

This classic game can be played on the blackboard or whiteboard.

Allow students to select a word and put in the dashes that match with the number of letters in the word. For example, a six-letter word should have six dashes on the board. The group need to guess a letter, one at a time. The teacher should explain about vowels and show them that it is best to use vowels in the first few guesses.

A correctly guessed letter goes above the dash. A letter that does not make up the word is recorded and the hangman's gibbet is started.

Can the word be guessed or will the victim die?

Note: To cut down the possibilities, ask them to select a famous actor or a pop group.

STARTER 2

The Blending Game

You need plenty of space.

Divide the group into two: A and B.

Stick the start of a word on a student's back (group A).

Stick the ending of the word on the backs of the other half (group B)

Each student has to find a matching partner to make up a complete word.

Here are some suggestions using 'est.'

Ch – est	B- est
T – est	L – est
W – est	R – est
V- est	P – est

You can also use 'ock'

Cl – ock	R – ock
Sh -ock	Bl – ock
T – ock	D – ock
S – ock	Fl – ock.

You can also use 'ap'

Ch – ap	Cl – ap
C – ap	Scr – ap
R – ap	M – ap.

Mixing the endings can vary the game.

Ch – est
Ch – ap = Chest/tap or chap/test.

Further spelling ideas

Turning Singular to Plural:

Point out to students that singular words can become plural by adding an 's' to the word.

Examples:

Apple – Apple<u>s</u>	Hand – Hand<u>s</u>
Finger – Finger<u>s</u>	Plum – Plum<u>s</u>
Thumb – Thumb<u>s</u>	Desk – Desk<u>s</u>

Point out that for some words that end in an x, students need to add an 'es'.

Examples:

Fox – Fox<u>es</u>	Box – Box<u>es</u>.

An 'es' is added for words ending in 'sh'.

Examples:

Bush – Bush<u>es</u>
Flush – Flush<u>es</u>
Dish – Dish<u>es</u>

Words that end in 'ch' also need an 'es'.

Lunch – Lunch<u>es</u>
Munch – Munch<u>es</u>
Punch – Punch<u>es</u>

A further variation of the blending game:

Group A can be the singular words and group B can be the plurals.

Half of group B can wear 's'; the other half can wear 'es'.

1 Recognise similar sounding words

Getting you thinking

Allow students to think of other words that sound the same but mean different things.

How does it work?

Explain that some words sound the same, are spelt the same, but mean different things.

Example: Ruler (king) Ruler (measuring tool.)

Now you try it

Students could work in small groups in this exercise.

Development

You may wish to photocopy the poem. Explain that sailor is written twice as it needs to be used twice in the poem. Explain that the poem rhymes so they are looking for pairs of words that rhyme.

2 Learn spellings

Getting you thinking

Model the **Look – 'Think' – Say – Cover – Write – Check** method by demonstrating the process. Then allow students to practise.

How does it work?

Allow students to use the method for themselves by following the process.

Now you try it

Make sure students use the method correctly.

Development

Tell students that when they come across a new word always use the LOOK – 'THINK' – SAY – COVER – WRITE – CHECK method to memorise it and that this is the most useful strategy they will ever learn for memorising new words. Tell students to:

- LOOK carefully at the new word. How can you break it into smaller bits? Do any of the smaller bits remind you of the patterns of letters from other words?

- 'THINK' about the parts of the words that might cause problems – double letters for instance, or a vowel that isn't pronounced as you would expect.

- SAY the word out loud or in your head.

- COVER the word and close your eyes. Try to see it in your mind's eye.

- WRITE the word down without looking back.

- CHECK to see if you're right. If not, look carefully at where you went wrong and try again.

More HOT TIPS for students

Whenever you have to copy a new word from the board, from a book or from a dictionary, always try to write the whole word in one go. Don't keep looking back after every few letters.

Try finger writing: while you're 'THINKing' about the word, pretend to write it with your finger, on your desk or on your hand.

Notes